THE DAWN ANIMAL AGENCY AND THE SANCTUARY FOR ANIMALS

SAFE IN THE SPOTLIGHT

THE DAWN ANIMAL AGENCY AND THE SANCTUARY FOR ANIMALS

SAFE IN THE SPOTLIGHT

WRITTEN BY

ELAINE SCOTT

PHOTOGRAPHS BY

MARGARET MILLER

MORROW JUNIOR BOOKS / NEW YORK

The text type is 14 point Berkeley Old Style Medium.

Additional photographs are reprinted by permission of *Newsweek* magazine (page 42, left) and photographer Jeff Mermelstein (page 45).
In addition, the Brook family very kindly shared their personal photographs on pages 25, 35, and 36 (top).

Library of Congress Cataloging-in-Publication Data
Scott, Elaine, 1940–
Safe in the spotlight: the Dawn Animal Agency and the Sanctuary for Animals/written by Elaine Scott; photographs by Margaret Miller.
p.   cm.
Summary: Explains how the Sanctuary for Animals and the Dawn Animal Agency hire out healthy animals for jobs in the performing arts and then use the money to support other animals who are too old or too sick to work themselves.
ISBN 0-688-08177-0 (trade).—ISBN 0-688-08178-9 (library) 1. Animal welfare—United States—Juvenile literature. 2. Working animals—United States—Juvenile literature. 3. Animals in television—United States—Juvenile literature. 4. Animals in motion pictures—United States—Juvenile literature. 5. Dawn Animal Agency—Juvenile literature. 6. Sanctuary for Animals—Juvenile literature. [1. Sanctuary for Animals. 2. Dawn Animal Agency. 3. Animal welfare. 4. Working animals. 5. Animals in motion pictures.] I. Miller, Margaret, 1945- ill. II. Title. HV4764.S36 1991 636.088'8—dc20 90-49677 CIP AC

Frontispiece: Phillip the camel waits to go on camera in Baltimore.

*This book is dedicated to
the memory of Joe,
and to the honor of all the other
animals at the Sanctuary*

Acknowledgments

The author and photographer wish to thank Leonard and Bunny Brook, Bambi and Amanda, Babette, and Neitcha for taking time from their busy days to answer questions and tell their stories. Thanks also go to Bob Daringer, Benjamin Williams, and Raul Gomez for sharing their knowledge with us—and rescuing the author when she got stuck in a muddy pasture!

Radio City Music Hall graciously allowed us to take photographs backstage during the Christmas Show, as did the New York City Opera during performances of *Mephisto*. Likewise, we want to thank the producers of *Avalon, Delirious,* and *Rude Awakening,* for permission to take photographs on the sets of those movies.

And the author wishes to express gratitude to Beverly Cleary, who came up with a title when everyone else was stumped; and to Margaret Miller, who made endless visits to various locations to catch the animals at work. To both of you, thank you, thank you—straight from the heart.

Introduction

"Easy, George, easy. Your turn is next. Bambi's done this dozens of times, and you know it doesn't hurt. Stand still, boy. Behave like the professional you are." Leonard Brook is looking up at his oldest camel while he talks to him in a gentle, soothing voice.

A few yards away, the noise of a vacuum cleaner pierces the early-morning quiet of the farm. Len's daughter Bambi is cleaning up Azuri, the youngest camel. The vacuum cleaner whirs as it runs over her soft brown coat, sucking out any loose tufts of fur. "No, no, Azuri," she says as she works. "You *cannot* suck my thumb. You're three years old now. It's time to give that up. C'mon, baby. I need to get you beautiful. You're working today."

Two other camels, Nora and Phillip, are waiting for their turn with the vacuum, while Len's wife, Bunny, gathers together an assortment of gilt-trimmed blankets. "Costumes are ready," she calls to her family as she heads toward the waiting trailer. Edith Ann, a crippled camel who cannot work, looks on sleepily, and why not? It's 6:30 in the morning, but the day has already begun at Wildflowers, home of the Sanctuary for Animals. Before they are ready to leave, Len, his family, and a few helpers will have vacuumed four camels and coaxed a tiger, two lions, a bear, and a jaguar into trailers. The animals have a job in a movie that begins filming in Baltimore this morning. Before they can leave for the long drive to Maryland, they must be groomed and fed.

Joe and Buttercup, two shaggy yellow dogs, look up eagerly as Len walks past, and he stops to scratch Joe behind an ear. "You guys are bums today," he says with a smile. "There's no work for you right now. Maybe next week. I *hope* you'll work next week. Dog food costs money." At the mention of dog food, Joe and Buttercup sniff the air expectantly. "Breakfast is coming," Len says. "Be patient."

Indeed, breakfast *is* coming—for all seven hundred animals who live with Len and Bunny Brook at their Sanctuary for Animals—and it takes everyone working together to get the job done.

Wildflowers, home of the Sanctuary for Animals is the name Len and Bunny have given to their property in Westtown, New York, a rural community just sixty-five miles north of New York City. The Brooks, along with Bambi and her daughter, Amanda, and family friends Ben Williams and Bob Daringer, live in a large white farmhouse that sits on one hundred acres of land. Most people have swing sets or barbecue pits in their backyards. The Brooks have lions, jaguars, tigers, and bears in theirs.

Actually, these animals do not have the run of the

Opposite: Bambi vacuums Azuri; and Baby, ready for work, gives a convincing snarl. Right: Ben Williams; below, Len Brook with Buttercup and Joe.

property. Instead, they live in their catteries well in back of the Brooks' house. Beyond the catteries lie the pen and sheds for the ostrich, kangaroos, and llamas. The pasture for the elephants stretches up the slight hill to the side of the ostrich pen. Across the road from the Brooks' house is another one hundred acres of farmland, with the barns and kennels for the rabbits, cats, and dogs. There are also pens for the chickens, pigeons, and turkeys, as well as a pond for the ducks. Goats and sheep graze in a separate area. There is a pasture on this side of the road, too, and it has been turned over to the camels, donkeys, cows, and horses. Seventy-five thousand dollars' worth of electric fencing keeps the animal population of the Sanctuary off the road and safe on their own property.

The catteries also have outdoor runs so that the animals can exercise.

Page 13: breakfast at the Sanctuary. Above: Amy Hyland. To the right: emus and chickens waiting to be fed. Opposite: Ben Daringer with a crowd of hungry goats, sheep, and donkeys.

When morning comes, everyone pitches in to see that the animals get fed. Tractors and trailors, four-wheel-drive vehicles, and wheelbarrows—all are used to haul food across the farm's acreage. Amy Hyland, a part-time employee, is often there at feeding time. The Brooks' other daughters, Babette and Neitcha, no longer live at the Sanctuary, but if they are visiting at home, they help, too. Each day the elephants, horses, camels, and donkeys eat four tons of hay. The Sanctuary's one hundred dogs gobble up their share of 250 pounds of dog food, and the bears eat the rest, along with a little fruit. The lions, tigers, jaguars, and cougars will finish off 150 pounds of meat, and then there are kangaroos, reindeer, ostrich, and emus, as well as the rats and mice, rabbits and pigeons, cows and pigs, sheep and goats, and cats to consider. All these creatures get hungry every single day, and the people at Wildflowers see to it that they are fed.

It wasn't always this way for these particular animals.

In the past, not all of them were fed when they were hungry or given enough food to satisfy them. Many were abandoned or abused by their former owners. For over thirty years now, the Brook family—along with a handful of loyal friends—have rescued creatures from slaughterhouses, from cruel treatment, and from abandonment.

Keeping so many animals safe and happy is exhausting and expensive work. The hay alone costs $120,000 a year. Len and Bunny do it willingly, because, as Len says, "All animals deserve a chance to live in peace." However, life is anything but peaceful for the Brooks as they work together to make their dream of providing a permanent home for abused animals a reality. This book will show you how the Dawn Animal Agency and the Sanctuary for Animals came to be.

A scene of contentment in one of the Sanctuary pastures. Opposite: Fritha, an Asian elephant that came to Wildflowers from Vietnam.

Leonard Brook was raised in New York City. When he was a boy, he didn't have a pet—not even a gerbil or a mouse, much less a dog or cat. He was interested in art, and thought he might want a career in government when he grew up. In fact, government was the subject he studied in college. Although he always loved animals, he never imagined that one day he would have hundreds of them in his care.

"Believe me, I never planned any of this," Len says with a laugh. "It all began when I met Bunny. Bunny has always had a soft spot for stray animals. When we met, she and her sister, Barbara Austin, had been taking in strays. At the time, they had twenty-eight dogs, nineteen cats, six rabbits, a capuchin monkey, and two ponies."

Len married Bunny, and the two of them continued to rescue animals that others either couldn't—or wouldn't—care for. George, one of the camels traveling to Baltimore this morning, has lived with Len and Bunny for almost thirty years. George was born in the middle of winter, and when he was two days old, his mother died. The small zoo where he was born simply couldn't take care of a baby camel that would have to be kept warm and fed with a bottle around the clock. Bunny heard about the situation. She and Len were willing to take care of the camel, and in no time they arrived at the zoo, loaded George into the back of their Volkswagen bus, and drove him home.

"We lived in a regular house in a regular neighborhood back in those days," Len says. "We weren't sure how the neighbors would feel about us keeping a camel in the backyard, so we tried to be kind of secretive about it. But camels make a funny noise. They sort of *moan*. Before long, the man who lived in back of us called and said, 'Do you guys have a camel over there?' We were almost afraid to say yes, but it turned out that he just wanted to come over and see it. He had been around camels when he served in the army, and he thought it was neat to have one living in the neighborhood."

Left: Bunny Brook. Opposite: Camels gather to inspect a tractor.

Although the neighbor didn't complain about George, Len knew that something was going to have to change. Large, exotic animals should never be raised as household pets. George couldn't grow up in a suburban backyard; he needed plenty of space to roam around. Len knew it was time to make some changes, so the Brooks bought a farm and moved themselves, their daughters, and their animals to it. The Sanctuary for Animals had been born. It was the beginning of a new life, and a new business, for all of them.

The population on their farm grew steadily as Len and Bunny kept on rescuing animals.

"It was just so hard to say no when we'd hear these pitiful stories," Len says. "For example, two of our earliest adoptions were Fjords—Norwegian workhorses—a mother and her foal, who was born blind. The horses' owner decided to get rid of them, so he took them to a livestock auction, where they were sold to two different meat-packers. That meant they would be turned into dog food. Naturally, the filly panicked when she was separated from her mother. She whinnied and threw herself about. Someone at the auction saw what was happening and called us. In order to persuade

them to sell, we offered each packer fifty dollars more than he had paid for the horse. It worked, and we brought the mare and her filly home to the Sanctuary. The reunion of mother and daughter was beautiful to watch—each of them nuzzling the other. A lot of our horses were rescued just as they were going to be sold for slaughter. Many of them were stable horses used for riding. Their owners sold them to packers after they became too old to be rented out for rides. That's an awful fate for a horse that has worked all its life. If we hear about it, we'll give them a home at the Sanctuary."

Animals come to the Sanctuary in other ways, as well. Sometimes Len and Bunny will buy animals, such as the Fjords, to save them from slaughter, but many times people just drop animals off at the Sanctuary in the middle of the night, then speed away. Skipper, a shaggy dog, arrived that way. "One morning, we found him tied to the fence. I don't understand how people can abandon a pet like that," Len says softly.

Occasionally, the ASPCA will remove animals from unfit homes. Someone in Staten Island had acquired a tiny lion cub, and, as often happens when people try to raise wild animals as pets, this person had no idea how to care for a lion that would eventually weigh four hundred pounds. The cub was ignored and chained in a dark and greasy garage, never seeing daylight. The

Page 22: Neitcha feeds a horse just rescued from slaughter. Opposite: Len with granddaughter Amanda. Top: Skipper. Right: Amanda and Meow as babies.

neighbors heard its cries and called the ASPCA. That organization took the cub away from its owner and asked Len, who has the proper facilities, to give the baby lion a home. When Meow was a cub, Len's granddaughter, Amanda, was allowed to pet her and play with her a bit—as long as an adult was around to supervise. Now that Meow is a fully grown lion, only adults who know how to handle her are allowed to work with her or pet her without supervision; but Meow is happy, and Amanda still can visit her in the cattery.

Of course, having the proper facilities to take care of animals that range from elephants to mice takes not only a lot of work but also a lot of money. It wasn't long after he moved to the Sanctuary that Len realized he was going to have to find a way to raise money if he wanted to keep on rescuing animals. As he pondered this problem, he noticed an advertisement in the newspaper. Someone needed a camel to be photographed for an advertising campaign. He had George! He called the people who had placed the ad, but they had already hired another camel. Although Len was disappointed, he made another important decision. He would form the Dawn Animal Agency. George and the other healthy animals would work and earn money to help support the Sanctuary animals who were too old, or too abused, to earn a living for themselves.

Pages 26 and 27: an African elephant with plenty of room to splash and cool off. Left: Len on the movie set of *Rude Awakening*. Opposite: Bambi backstage with cast members of the New York City Opera.

From the beginning, Len knew the work would be difficult, but he was determined to succeed—and on his own terms. "Many animal talent agencies care only about the money," Len says. "They'll trip animals, or poke them; sometimes they beat them to get them to perform. It's outrageous. I've heard of agencies that will 'adopt' kittens from a shelter, use them in a commercial, then return them to the shelter when they're finished earning money from them. Since we believe in neutering all of the animals at the Sanctuary, we might adopt kittens from a shelter, too, if we get a job that calls for them. But all of our adoptions are permanent. An animal that comes to us has a loving home with us forever. And that is true whether the animal works or not."

When his animals are working, Len insists that someone from the Sanctuary, or from the Dawn Animal Agency, be with them at all times. As he says, "We never send them off to a job by themselves, because we are the ones who look after their safety and their comfort."

Nevertheless, Len is quick to point out that the people who hire his animals are not cruel. These people produce commercials, movies, or plays for a living. Some of them work for advertising agencies. Few know any-

Len working with a Dawn performer.

Above: Amanda on the tractor with Ben Williams. Opposite: Bob Daringer takes a break.

thing about properly caring for animals that work in show business, and the animals can suffer because of ignorance, not cruelty. For example, the lights on a television or movie set are very bright and very hot. Young kittens could become dehydrated and die if they were left unattended—even for a lunch break. Someone from the Sanctuary is there to protect the Dawn animals when others don't know enough to move them out of harm's way.

The Sanctuary for Animals is a kind of sanctuary for

people, too. As Babette says, laughing, "Mother takes in people the same way she takes in animals!" People used to working with animals—especially those who have worked for circuses, carnivals, or wild-animal shows—know about the Brooks' work. Between jobs, these people often show up at the Sanctuary, offering to stay and help for a while. Sometimes the stay lasts a few months; sometimes it lasts for years.

Ben Williams has been working at the Sanctuary for nearly thirty years now. He's just like a member of the family. Bob Daringer is like family, too. He had a business of his own—painting stripes on the highway—but he always had a soft spot in his heart for the animals and found time to "help out," as he says, whenever he could. Now that he has sold his business, Bob has moved to Wildflowers and devotes all his time to the animals.

And with seven hundred of them to care for, help is always needed!

Like the Fjords, many of the animals came to the Sanctuary straight from the auction block. Animals are sold at auction for many different reasons. Exotic animals, such as lions and tigers, are sometimes sold to people who ship them to their private ranches, then invite hunters to come shoot them—for a fee.

Bunny Brook often goes to animal auctions to see whether there are animals she can rescue. When Neitcha was a little girl, Bunny went to an auction where twenty healthy ostrich chicks were for sale—along with one featherless chick, too sick to hold its head up. Bunny knew what fate awaited the sick ostrich, so she bought it and took it back to the Sanctuary. She moved it into the house and began to nurse it back to health. First, she cut up one of Neitcha's snowsuits to protect the chick and keep it warm. Then she coaxed it to eat. For a while, it was touch and go. No one thought the baby ostrich would live. However, that was ten years ago, and now Big Bird is a healthy, happy four-hundred-pound ostrich that can look forward to living another fifty years or so at Wildflowers, her home.

Babette, who lives in New York City now, remembers her childhood and says, "It was wonderful, but it was also a lot of work. Mother taught us from the beginning that these were wild animals, not toys. She made sure we understood what they could do—even accidentally—and she did her best to keep us from getting into situations where we could get hurt."

When Babette's younger sister Neitcha was a child, one of her best friends was a baboon named Ea! Ea! Ea! Len says the baboon got her name from the sound she made. Under Bunny's careful eye, Neitcha and Ea! Ea! Ea! played together as equals, and on occasion the baboon would carefully groom her human friend.

Amanda is growing up at the Sanctuary now, and she is learning the same lesson that the Brooks' daughters learned. Although it is great fun to have animals to play with, it is important to treat them with respect and

Opposite: Greta the cougar came to Wildflowers from a bankrupt circus. Below: Bob with a thriving Big Bird. Right: Neitcha as a child with Ea! Ea! Ea!

remember that they are not toys. And it isn't all play. Even at her young age, Amanda helps out whenever she can. When Wilbur was a piglet, Amanda fed him his bottle. Now Wilbur is a 130-pound adolescent pig that loves to romp and play with the dogs. Eventually, Wilbur will weigh in at 500 pounds. Although he would not want to hurt Amanda, Wilbur's weight alone could make him dangerous to a young child. You can look for Wilbur in a recent Bob Dylan music video. He is wearing a gold ring in his nose as he rides in the backseat of a limousine. Len is quick to point out that Wilbur's nose is not pierced and that the ring does not hurt him!

The Brook family is determined to see that the animals are cared for in the future as well as now. They want to be certain that the work of the Sanctuary for Animals and Dawn Animal Agency will go on, even if they are not able to supervise it. Len says, "After all, some of my animals will live to be senior citizens. George is already thirty, but Azuri is only a baby; she's three. The elephants aren't quite twenty, and they'll live to be sixty-five or so. So will Big Bird. I won't be around, but some of the animals will be here when Amanda grows up. I

Amanda with Wilbur as a piglet (above) and hugging a miniature horse (below). Opposite: Bambi takes the adolescent Wilbur for a walk.

had to find a way to keep the Sanctuary going after Bunny and I are gone."

In order to do this, Len decided to turn the Sanctuary for Animals into a nonprofit corporation. Unlike small businesses such as your local shoe store or cleaner, a corporation is a business that has more than one owner and therefore can easily continue to exist after the founder of the company wishes to retire, or dies. People buy shares of stock in the corporation and become part owners, sharing in the business's profits, or losses. However, a nonprofit corporation does not try to earn money. Instead, it relies on donations and fund-raising activities in order to get enough money to continue its work. The

government has strict rules that apply to both profit and nonprofit corporations, so one of the first things Len had to do in order to incorporate the Sanctuary was to establish a board of trustees.

The board of trustees in any corporation is very powerful. It sets the policies, or rules, by which the business will be run. The board of trustees can even hire and fire the president of the company! Len and Bunny wanted people on the Sanctuary's board who understood what it takes to run a business but who also understood their love of animals. They carefully chose eight people to serve as trustees. Ben Williams is a trustee, and so is Barbara Austin, who, along with Bunny, started the whole thing by rescuing strays so long ago. If anything happens to the Brooks, the board of trustees will see to it that the work of the Sanctuary for Animals, Inc., continues.

Many times, nonprofit corporations will have an advisory board. Members of the advisory board don't vote at the regular board meetings, but they lend their help in other ways, such as raising funds or getting publicity for the organization. Willard Scott, Ed Asner, and Joanne Woodward are some of the celebrities who have agreed to serve on the advisory board of the Sanctuary for Animals, Inc.

The Dawn Animal Agency is a corporation, too. Since

it charges fees for the animals to perform, it cannot be a nonprofit corporation. Of course, all the money the animals earn through the agency goes right back to the Sanctuary, to support the hundreds of animals who cannot work. There is never any extra money, and Len and Bunny always worry about having enough funds to keep the Sanctuary going.

Opposite: Bambi backstage at the New York City Opera. Left: Meow performs as a circus lion, and below, Babette prepares to lead a horse on to the stage of Radio City Music Hall.

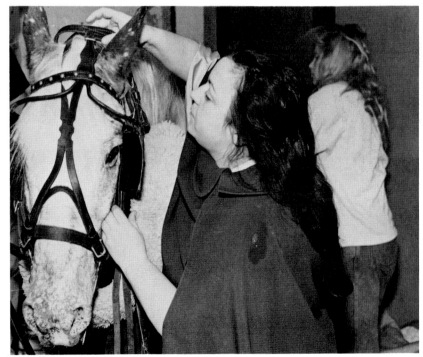

The working animals at the Sanctuary have many different assignments. Chickens, ducks, goats, dogs, camels, and horses all have work they can do. Some appear in movies. George appeared in a music video with the stars of *Ishtar*—Dustin Hoffman and Warren Beatty—and Joe, who is a real celebrity, was a guest on David Letterman's show. Still others do "print work"; that is, they pose for photographs that are run in magazines and newspapers. Joe and David Letterman were photographed together for the cover of *Newsweek*. Ninja, a jaguar, posed for a blue-jean ad, and a turkey that Len took in when its young owner had to get rid of it appeared in a Pepperidge Farm commercial.

THE OIL BUST: END OF A CARTEL?

Newsweek

February 3, 1986 · $2.00

Staying Up Late With Letterman

All of the animal actors are trained for their jobs by a member of Len's "family"—someone who is associated with the Sanctuary or Dawn Animal Agency. Raul Gomez, a former circus worker, is a person who has worked with Len off and on for years. Raul is very good with the camels—and with the lambs. "I don't do this for the money," Raul says. "It's my contribution. When a small circus folds, Len will take its animals and give them a good home. Everyone in the circus world knows the people at the Sanctuary really care about animals."

Jasmine, a gentle, semiblind tiger, came to the Sanctuary from a circus. When the circus was sold to a group of people in Mexico, the wife of the circus owner was worried about Jasmine. She had raised the tiger by hand since it was a cub, and she didn't think Jasmine would adjust well to the new owners and a new life in Mexico. The woman realized she couldn't keep the tiger, but, like Raul, she also knew about the Sanctuary for Animals. She asked the Brooks to give Jasmine a home, and they did. From time to time, Jasmine still performs, but

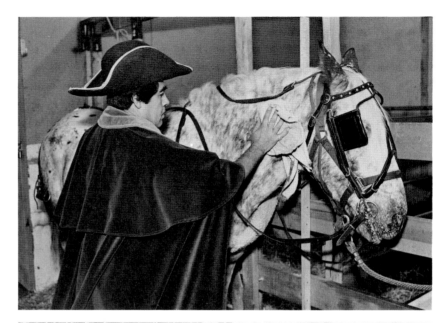

Page 40: Len and an assistant with Ninja the jaguar on a fashion shoot. Opposite page: Joe and television personality David Letterman on the cover of *Newsweek* (left) and a turkey that posed for Pepperidge Farm (right). Above: Raul Gomez costumed for the Radio City Music Hall Christmas show. Below: Jasmine gets a gentle stroke from Amy Hyland.

Ernie Karpeles with Bean. Opposite: Bean at work.

Sherri Kaizerman with Sinatra.

she's not working as hard now as she did when she was with the circus.

When the animals work, they get their jobs through the Dawn Animal Agency, which is located in New York City. Barbara Austin runs the agency, and she is helped by Ernie Karpeles and Sherri Kaizerman. Ernie has a degree in biology and worked at zoos in Europe for a while after he graduated from college, and Sherri worked in Hawaii, doing research with dolphins. Although they didn't know each other, it turns out they grew up in the same Philadelphia neighborhood. Eleven years ago, they both came to work for Dawn.

Barbara, Ernie, and Sherri schedule all the animals' jobs, train some of them, and accompany them to work. A few of the domestic cats make their home at Dawn, while others live at the Sanctuary. Ernie says, "Each of us has our favorite cat among the ones who live here. Bean is mine, and Sinatra is Sherri's."

Bean is an eleven-year-old calico who, Ernie says, "is the most photographed cat in America, and she's sweet and smart. She'll sit and stay on command, just like a dog does." Bean has appeared on posters, boxes of cat food, and in movies. Perhaps you saw her in *Heaven Help Us, Moscow on the Hudson,* or *Garbo Talks*. Maybe you saw her dressed up as a tourist, posing with her canine husband on a Purina poster that Ernie says was hung in veterinary offices all over the country.

Sinatra is eight years old, and he has appeared in

Revlon ads, several movies (including *Garbo Talks*, with Bean), and in a Black & Decker commercial for its Dustbuster vacuum cleaner.

Dawn Animal Agency exists to help the Sanctuary for Animals. The Sanctuary does not exist to provide animal performers for Dawn. Unlike other animal actors and models, Sanctuary animals work for one reason only: to earn money to support the "freeloaders," as Len affectionately calls the nonworking animals.

Ernie is full of admiration for the Brook family. He says, "Once they saw how much money Dawn Animal Agency made with the working animals, the Brooks could have gotten rid of all the other ones, and been millionaires. But they didn't do that. They're dedicated people, dedicated to all the animals."

The days are busy at Dawn and at the Sanctuary. When there is a bit of time to spare, training is squeezed in. Ernie and Sherri like to work with the cats; Bunny is an expert on the elephants; Bambi loves the horses; and Len especially likes to work with the dogs—particularly Joe.

Joe was starved and covered with mange when a humane-society worker from Brooklyn took him to the

Opposite: Sherri and Ernie with two lively Dawn performers. Left: Bambi with a Sanctuary kangaroo.

Sanctuary. Len nursed Joe back to health, then began working with him to teach him simple commands. "It wasn't hard to teach Joe," Len says. "He's intelligent, friendly, and anxious to please. Everyone who meets him loves him."

Len says the hardest command to teach a dog is "Go!"

"Dogs are social," he says. "Their instinct is to come to you. They'll sit, lie down, roll over, anything that keeps them near you. But go? That's hard."

Len with Joe on a movie set.

Cain came to the Sanctuary when a small game park closed down. So did his owner, Mike Metzger.

Len was on a movie set with several of his goats, sheep, and dogs as he talked about training, and Joe wandered over. "Joe, go!" Len commanded, motioning the dog back to where the director waited for him. Joe cocked an ear at Len, hesitated for just a second, then went back to finish his work. Len watched as Joe trotted away. "Such a smart dog," he said with satisfaction.

Len collected Cain right away, but it took Mike a few weeks to begin work at the Sanctuary.

Now, whenever Cain sees Len, he lets out a king-of-the-jungle roar! Len says, "Cain has never forgiven me for separating him from Mike."

There is a difference between training animals and handling them. Training an animal means teaching it something, such as a new trick. Handling an animal means you manage to control it. Len says, "You train a dog, but you handle a chicken, or a lion."

Regardless of whether they are training or handling the Sanctuary animals, everyone involved treats them with care and understanding. No one uses punishment to teach the animals to obey.

Even animals that are treated with kindness sometimes require medical care. Like humans, animals must have their innoculations against disease. If they become sick or injured, they must see a veterinarian.

However, it is one thing to take a sick dog or cat to

Above: Dr. Ahmed Abdur-Razzaq greets Azuri. Right and opposite: The veterinarian and Bunny Brook examine Fritha and an African elephant.

the vet and quite another to take a sick camel or elephant! The Sanctuary is fortunate to have a veterinarian, Dr. Ahmed Abdur-Razzaq, who will make house calls. Dr. Abdur-Razzaq is very interested in the Sanctuary, and he makes a tremendous contribution to the animals' health and happiness. Although the veterinarian goes to the Sanctuary regularly, all of the Brooks know how to give the animals rabies shots, painkillers, and other medications.

At the Sanctuary, Bambi and sometimes Neitcha take care of the horses, and Bunny is an expert on the exotic animals—especially the elephants. Bunny has become so knowledgeable that veterinarians from around the country consult her if they are treating an elephant with a problem that has them stumped. In fact, a veterinarian who was stationed in Vietnam with the U.S. Army came across an Asian elephant that had been burned and scarred with napalm. He knew about Bunny's expertise and got in touch with her to see whether she would give the elephant a home. Of course, the answer was yes, and Fritha made the journey across half a world to live in peace at Wildflowers.

The Brooks' care and understanding extends beyond mere kindness. It affects the way they live their lives. No one at the Sanctuary would think of eating meat. Everyone living there is a vegetarian. And as far as fur coats are concerned, the Brooks have one word for them: *abominations!* Len says, "Men no longer need to kill animals to keep warm."

Raul Gomez has said, "Once you take an animal into captivity, it is totally dependent on you. In a way, that puts you in captivity, too. People need to think about this when they decide to keep any animals—even a dog or a cat or a goldfish." Many of the inhabitants of the Sanctuary for Animals are there because their original

Amanda is a third-generation worker at the Sanctuary. Opposite: Bambi exercises a favorite horse, Snow, in preparation for a real-life wedding in which the bride will ride to the ceremony sidesaddle.

owners were not willing to be responsible for them.

Most of the time, people ask the Sanctuary to accept animals, but occasionally there are offers to adopt one. With all those hungry mouths to feed each day, one would think the Brooks would answer, "Gladly!" They don't, however. Once an animal goes to the Sanctuary, it has a home there until it dies. The Brooks don't do adoptions because they do not have the time it would take to check out each prospective home. As they say, "We would never place an animal in a home we didn't know."

Because the Sanctuary always needs money, every job the animals get is important. Therefore, as long as he knows the animals will be safe and not hurt, Len accepts a variety of assignments for them, from posing for advertising photographs to appearing in major motion pictures, operas, and Broadway plays.

Each job has its problems. For a television commercial, Len had to coax several of his chickens to wear tiny bikinis, beach hats, and terry-cloth robes. "I had a problem with the beach hats. The wardrobe lady had to redo them because they wouldn't fit comfortably over the chickens' combs," Len says.

Page 54: a Dawn performer with a cast member of the New York City Opera. This page and opposite: at work on the movie *Rude Awakening*.

For another job, a movie called *Rude Awakening,* the chickens were to appear in their natural feathered state. However, their scene was being filmed outdoors, and Len had to keep a constant count of them, since one kept disappearing into the surrounding bushes.

"Bwaak, bwaak, bwaak, bwaak," Len called over and over again as he searched for his missing chicken.

"I'd make chicken soup out of that one," one of the cameramen said after Len had been looking for several minutes.

"That's not funny," Len answered coldly.

Eventually, the chicken reappeared and was carefully placed in the coop. Len's chickens, goats, and dogs all had work in that particular movie However, like actors everywhere, these animals run the risk that their scenes will be cut from the movie before it is released to the public. That's what happened with *Rude Awakening.* As they say in show business, the animals' scenes "hit the cutting-room floor."

For years now, Len has provided the animals for the Radio City Music Hall Christmas Show. One year, twelve animals—three camels (Azuri, Debbie, and Phillip), a horse (Alfie), two donkeys, four sheep, and two lambs (four-month-old Norton and eight-week-old Maggie May)—traveled to Manhattan for the duration of the show.

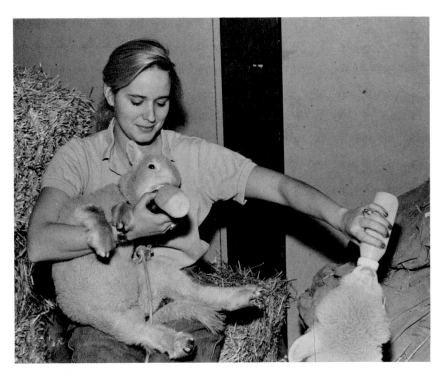

Basement quarters beneath Radio City Music Hall. Above: A helper feeds Norton and Maggie May. Right: Donkeys wait patiently to go onstage. Opposite page: Raul Gomez and Phillip.

Doing live theater with these animals can have its drawbacks. The Christmas Show runs for nine weeks, and there are up to five performances a day. The animals live in the basement of the giant music hall, and people from the Sanctuary live right there with them. The famous dancers, the Rockettes, have to get used to waiting their turn for the elevators while the camels and horses

Above: horse and helper emerging from the elevator, ready to perform. Opposite: Maggie May goes for a walk and waits quietly near the Rockettes' costume rack.

use them to get to their places, ready to make their entrance onstage.

The youngest member of the animal entourage, Maggie May, got restless during the long Nativity tableau. She was supposed to lie down and be good while the narrator told the Christmas story. Unfortunately, she decided it was time to act like a baby lamb, and she got up and frisked around the stage, drawing a lot of attention to herself. When that show was over, a phone call came from the director. "Do something with that lamb! I want it to lie down for the next show!"

Raul Gomez, who was handling Maggie May, got an

idea. "Let's go for a walk, girl," he said. Raul put a collar and leash on Maggie May and took her out on the sidewalks of New York City. Around and around the block, he and Maggie May walked. People, busy with their Christmas shopping, stopped to stare.

"What *is* that?" one woman asked.

"A poodle," answered her companion.

"No, it's a lamb," said another passerby. "Imagine that, a lamb in New York City! I'd like to buy her for my grandchild."

"She's not for sale," Raul answered firmly.

When Maggie May returned to Radio City after her walk, she was tired and ready for a nap. Raul gave her

a bottle, and she slept through the next show, just as the director wanted.

While Maggie May has yet to learn how to perform, Len has many animals that are real show-business professionals. Kisser, a goat, has appeared in the Houston Grand Opera's touring company of *Porgy and Bess;* various horses work with the New York City Opera Company; and eight dogs, including Skipper, recently worked with John Candy as he filmed a movie in New York City. The dogs were supposed to snatch a bag of doughnuts from Mr. Candy and run away. In order to entice them to do that correctly, Bambi told the production assistants to smear a bit of baby food on the bottom of the doughnut bag. It worked like a charm.

Opposite: The Radio City Music Hall Christmas show. This page: Kisser, a stage veteran.

On location with the movie *Delirious*, Sherri Kaizerman confers with a production assistant (above) and works with one of the Dawn performers (right). Opposite: Bambi, playing a dog walker, will soon collide with actor John Candy.

In Len's opinion, all of his animal actors are stars—from the pigeons that flew overhead in *Ghostbusters* to the dogs, including Joe and Buttercup, who performed in *Moonstruck*. Len says, "These are animals working to support other animals, not humans." Sanctuary animals work hard, but they are happy, healthy—and loved.

Dawn Animal Agency charges a minimum of four hundred dollars to take an animal to a job—even if it's a small animal, such as a mouse.

"There has to be a minimum charge, because of insurance and traveling and handling costs," Len says.

Azuri earns seven hundred dollars a day, while Sinatra or Bean may get four hundred. When the bears and lions and tigers work, each can earn two thousand dollars. Of course, out of that, Len must pay for the trucks that transport the animals, the gasoline, the insurance (on the animals themselves and on any damage they might accidentally do to property or people), plus food and lodging for the handlers, if they are going to be away overnight.

At the beginning of this book, it was 6:30 in the morning. Len and Bambi were getting Azuri, George, Nora, and Phillip vacuumed and ready to go to work. The camels, along with Jasmine the tiger, lions Baby and Meow, a bear named Hubba, and Ninja the jaguar, are going to Baltimore, where producer Barry Levinson is filming his new movie. Mr. Levinson remembers a circus parade that passed down one particular street in Baltimore when he was a child, and now he wants to re-create the parade for his movie. He has hired Dawn Animal Agency to provide the animals. It is a very big job, and Len is happy. He just hopes that nothing goes wrong. The Sanctuary needs the money these animals will make.

Plans are made that Babette, Bambi, and Neitcha, along with Amanda, will drive the big cats and the bear to Baltimore. Instead of using his own elephants, Len has contracted with a circus closer to Baltimore to use theirs. Although the circus will take the elephants to Baltimore, Len will be responsible for them while they work. Len and a helper named Nick Giordano will take George, Azuri, Phillip, and Nora with them. As the sun rises, all of the animals are on their way.

When Len and Nick arrive in Baltimore, the elephants are already on the set, where the filming takes place. In this case, the set is the Baltimore neighborhood where

Page 66: on location with Barry Levinson's *Avalon*. Opposite: Len loads hay for the journey to Baltimore. Above: The camels arrive!

Barry Levinson grew up. The movie company has taken over at least two blocks of it, closing the streets to traffic. Apparently, some of the residents of the neighborhood were unaware that a movie was going to be filmed there. They are very surprised to wake up and find elephants lying on their sidewalks, getting brushed off. When Len and Nick arrive, the camels are taken out of the trailer and given fresh hay and water.

A car crawls slowly down the street, and Len speaks to one of the production company assistants. "This street is supposed to be closed to cars. It's dangerous for the animals," he says, and the assistant hurries off to be certain the police barricades are in place.

Len and Nick sort through the various blankets that Bunny put in the trailer. They will be draped over the camels, and the men choose blankets that will look just

right on each. Since Len and Nick will be leading the camels in the parade, a person from wardrobe brings each of them a costume, too—a khaki uniform and hat. As the man tries to put a tie on Len, Azuri comes up and nuzzles him, asking for affection.

"I've never been kissed by a camel before," he says, smiling.

It is mid-morning now, and Babette and her sisters have not arrived. Len is beginning to wonder where they are, and he slips away to call Bunny, who is back at the Sanctuary. She tells him they left hours ago.

The director wants to begin rehearsing the parade, even though the cats are missing. Len looks at the elephants. "Time to go to work, you guys," he says. "Tails. Tails."

Each elephant uses his trunk to grab the tail of the elephant in front of him, and off they go to the next block, where the filming is taking place. Another handler goes with them, and as they round the corner, you can hear him saying, "Slow, slow. Tails, tails."

Len and Nick come next. Len is leading Azuri, who looks as if she is enjoying the whole thing. "C'mon, little girl," he says. "C'mon."

Opposite: An elephant prepares to face the camera. This page: Len gets into costume for the parade.

Neighbors pour from their houses, holding children and grandchildren. "Look at that!" they exclaim. "Look at those animals!"

The morning crawls by, and the parade is rehearsed over and over again. Between rehearsals, Len and Nick answer the neighbors' questions, pose for pictures, and let the children pet the animals. Len is worried, though. Where are his daughters? Where are the other animals? Another phone call back to the Sanctuary reveals that the women have phoned home, saying they are having

Pages 72 and 73: The parade passes by. Above: Baby's work is done. Opposite: Amanda and Bambi after a long day.

mechanical trouble with the truck that pulls the trailer. Everyone hopes it will be fixed in time to get the animals to Baltimore before the sun goes down. If they don't show up today, they will lose their chance to be in this movie, and the Sanctuary will lose the money they would have earned.

Finally, at 6:00 P.M., the truck arrives. Baby and Meow, Jasmine, Hubba, and Ninja are quickly transferred to circus wagons, and the parade passes by once again. The movie cameras roll, and everyone breathes a sigh of relief.

At last, the director is happy with the shot and he calls for a "wrap," which means that the filming is finished for the day. The animals are walked back to their trailers. They have been working—or traveling—all day and are tired. Bambi, Babette, Neitcha, and Amanda are tired, too. Amanda is hungry, and asks her mother for a sandwich. After she's eaten it, mother and daughter rest on the curb.

The animals are hungry, too, and Len puts out fresh hay and water for the elephants and camels, and fresh meat for the rest. Neighborhood children gather around for one last look. One father asks whether he can put his child on Azuri's back just for a minute to take a picture. Len is pleasant but firm when he refuses. "She's tired now, and she needs to rest. You can feed her some hay, but no sitting on her back."

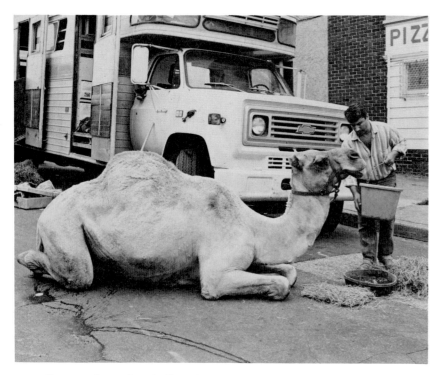

A well-earned rest for Phillip, above, and Azuri. Opposite: home at last.

As the sky grows dark, the animals once again are loaded onto their trailers and pulled to the hotel. A few adults will spend the night outside with the animals, while others will get some sleep in the hotel beds. Today the camels, big cats, and bear have been in the spotlight. Tomorrow they will begin the long drive north to West-town and the peace and quiet of Wildflowers. By to-morrow night, everyone—animals and people—will be safe at home.

Author's Note

The Brooks' dream of animals working to support other animals has come true. However, the Sanctuary for Animals still needs help. All contributions to it are tax-deductible and go to help the Brooks rescue more animals. Contributions should be made out to:

The Sanctuary for Animals, Inc.
William Lain Road
Westtown, New York 10998